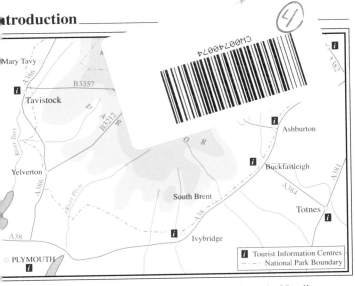

Mary Tavy
B3357
Tavistock
Yelverton
River Tavy
B3212
River Plym
DARTMOOR
QR
South Brent
A38
Ivybridge
Ashburton
Buckfastleigh
Totnes
A384
A381
A382
PLYMOUTH

CJW007400074

i Tourist Information Centres
- - - National Park Boundary

Dartmoor is an area of high moorland, approximately 20 miles (30kms) from west to east and a little under 30 miles (50kms) from north to south. It is a cap of granite thrusting up from the surrounding Devon farmland, covered by peat, moss, grass and heather. At its highest point – High Willhays, near Okehampton – it rises to 2,039ft (621m) above sea level, but most of the moorland is high enough to be plagued by a great feature of the area – the mist which rolls in from the nearby sea. Walkers will find this mist a considerable challenge, and must have a good grasp of navigation if they are to avoid becoming lost when walking on the moor.

This guide describes walks on and around the southern half of Dartmoor: ie, south of a line crossing east-west slightly to the north of Tavistock. A glance at the map will show that there is a natural division around this point – the line of the River Dart – and a man-made division – the ragged saltire of B-roads crossing the moor. The bulk of the highest ground on the moor is to the north of this line, but there is a lower moorland plateau to the south, with a mass of rivers – arranged like the spokes of a wheel – carrying the high rainfall from the tops.

This rainfall is captured in reservoirs, which are a feature of a number of the walks in this guide: the pleasant woodland around Burrator Reservoir (*Walks 9,10*); the bleak moorland at Avon Dam (*16,17*) and the conifer wood around tiny Venford Reservoir (*21*).

On the high moor, near the junction of the two roads crossing the moor (the B3212 and the B3357) is the village of Princetown, with its famous prison. There is also a National Park information centre (the High Moorland Visitor Centre) and some fine walking over the adjacent moors (*6,7*). Nearby is Foxtor Mires – thought to have been the inspiration for the most famous fictional representation of Dartmoor: Grimpen Mire in Conan Doyle's *The Hound of the Baskervilles*.

Navigation around the moor by car is fairly straightforward. The city of Plymouth sits to the south-west, with the A386 leading north, through Yelverton, Horrabridge (*13*) and the handsome market town of Tavistock, and the A38 heading east, to Ivybridge (*18*), then northeast by Buckfastleigh and Ashburton. There is a network of small roads in the far east of the moor, but otherwise access is only by the two roads crossing the moor or by foot.

Once walking on the moor you will encounter a number of distinctive features.

Tors: These are outcrops of weathered and broken granite – usually on hilltops. Over millennia, ice, frost, wind and rain has worn them into fantastic shapes. They can be found in similar landscapes throughout Britain, but are particularly common on Dartmoor. Half of

the walks in this guide pass a significant tor, but Great Mis Tor (*4*) and Vixen Tor (private, but you can get a good view of it) (*5*) are particularly striking.

Archaeology: Due to the durability of the local granite and the lack of intensive

Vixen Tor (see Walk 5)

and-use on the moor, Dartmoor has the largest concentration of early archaeological remains in the country. From the Neolithic and Bronze Age periods there are a mass of cairns (there are splendid examples on Corndon Down (*22*)), stone circles (*3*) and standing stones and stone rows (*9,14*). Above all, there are literally thousands of round Bronze Age huts. Most nowadays are little more than a raised circle in the ground, but the huts on Harford Moor still give a good idea of the layout of a Bronze Age settlement (*19*).

Spurrell's Cross (see Walk 19)

Crosses: Free-standing stone crosses were erected on the moor over many centuries. They have no single purpose: some appear to mark boundaries; others roads; some may be memorials. Today, in misty weather, they can be a very useful navigational aid. You will pass several on the walks in this guide; notably Cadover Cross (*15*), Spurrell's Cross (*19*) and Siward's/Nun's Cross (*7,9*) – the largest cross on the moor.

Mines: Throughout the area you will find evidence of tin mining, which has been carried out on Dartmoor since before the Romans arrived. Many of the works are now little more than scrapes and mounds, but the mines which were worked into the 19th century were larger and care must be taken around the excavations. The most obvious of these mines is at Eylesbarrow (*14*).

Warrens: Commercial rabbit warrens existed on the marginal land of Dartmoor for several centuries. Their existence is remembered both in place names and in the areas of 'pillow mounds' – small artificial hillocks built to give the rabbits dry ground in which to burrow. Examples can be seen around Ditsworthy Warren (*14*) and Huntingdon Warren, above Avon Dam Reservoir (*17*).

Leats: These are man-made water channels, and you will come across them all over Dartmoor. Some were for drinking-water supplies; some to power mills; and others were used in the tin mining industry. In each case, they took water from one place and carried it across the slope to where it was needed. Many are now little more than dry ditches, but the most important – the Devonport Leat – is still flowing. This was built between the 16th and 18th centuries to provide water for the growing population of the naval base and city of Plymouth (7,10).

Ponies: There have been wild ponies in this area for thousands of years, and they have been domesticated since before records began. The Dartmoor Pony – small and hardy – is a specific breed (though other breeds may be seen on the moor). They are the property of the Dartmoor commoners and are likely to be met grazing on many of the walks in this guide. They are generally friendly but should not be approached or fed.

Artillery Ranges

The Ministry of Defence maintains three large sections of the north of Dartmoor as live firing ranges: Okehampton Range, Willsworthy Range and Merrivale Range. As all three are north of the B3357 they only just touch on the routes in this book (Walks *1*, *2* and *4* are near Merrivale Range; Walk *3* enters it), but it is important to understand how they work in case you extend your walking on the moor.

Boundary Pole

The boundaries of the ranges are marked by lines of red and white posts, taller than a man. The public is allowed to walk within these areas provided they are not being used for live firing. When they are being used, large red flags are displayed in prominent positions (red lights at night). Alternatively, the firing programme is listed in advance on the internet (currently at **www.dartmoor-ranges.co.uk**).

Although firing is now restricted to the designated areas, the whole of Dartmoor has been used in the past (notably during World War II). As a result, there is a slight chance of discovering old ordnance lying anywhere on the moor. If you find anything which looks suspicious, avoid touching it and report it as soon as possible.

Warning Flag

circuit on tracks and paths through grazing land, leading to a tor.
ngth: **5 miles/8km**; *Height Climbed:* **720ft/220m**. *Possible link with*
lk 2.

O.S. Sheet OL28

Stephen's Grave

reach the start of this walk, drive
miles north from Tavistock on the
386 and turn right (east) on the mi-
r road to Peter Tavy. Drive through
e village, past the church, then first
ght beyond. Drive up this narrow
ad until there are fields to the left as
ell as right. When the fields to the
ft end there is a car park to the left.

Walk out of the car park and
rn left up the road. After a short
stance a sign points left for the
ath to White Tor. Follow this track,
rough bracken at first, then along
walled lane. The wall ends to the
ght, then the left. At this point there
a crossroads, marked by the stone
Stephen's Grave. Keep straight
n at the moment, to explore the tor,
on Age fort and cairns on White
r, visible ahead, then double back
the crossroads. Turn left here (ie,
rn right, if you are walking in the
riginal direction), past the grave.

The grassy path leads you gently
downhill to a wall. Go left along this.
Ignore the gate leading into a field
above Wedlake and continue. The
wall goes right and leads you down
to a corner. Ford a stream and go
through a gate beyond.

Head half-right across the field
(sign) to reach a gate in the top corner. Beyond this you are on the open,
grassy moor. Continue in the same
direction to reach the corner of a wall,
then follow the wall across the slope.

Continue in this direction until you
join a metalled road. Turn right down
this to reach Higher Godsworthy
Farm. Walk through the farm buildings (dogs on leads) and on down the
metalled access road beyond.

As you approach Lower Godsworthy a path (which can be very wet)
heads off to the left. Follow this to
join the public road beyond the farm.
Turn left to return to the start.

2 Cox Tor

A short circuit, with a moderate climb to a low tor. Grassy paths and a quiet public road. Length: 3¹/₂ miles/5.6km; Height Climbed: **390ft/120m**. *Possible link with Walk 1.*

O.S. Sheet OL

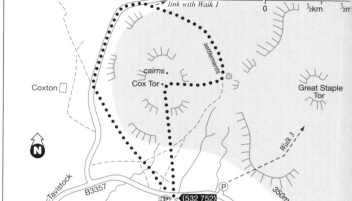

To reach the start of this walk drive 2¹/₂ miles east from Tavistock on the B3357. Shortly after the road emerges from fields onto the open moor there is a large car park to the right of the road.

Cross the road and directly ahead of you is Cox Tor, with a rocky top and a clear path leading directly to it. Climb to the top, explore the mass of rocks and enjoy the views.

Looking east from the top (ie, to the right as you are climbing) you will see a small tarn on the grassy col between Cox Tor and Great Staple Tor. Walk down to this on a rough sheep path. On the near side of the tarn turn left, on a rough path. This passes through the remains of the circular huts of ancient settlements as it winds round the back of the hill. The path is unclear in places – don't worry: jut keep going round the hill (ie, not down the shallow valley to your right) until a narrow public road becomes visible below. Drop down join this and turn left along it (to link with Walk 1 go right).

Continue along this pleasant, unfenced road until, above Coxton farm, a rough path heads off through the bracken to the left, marked by a yellow arrow.

The path contours round the hill. As it nears the road other paths head off to right and left. Keep straight on, aiming for the highest point of the road ahead, to return to the car park.

Roos Tor _____ B

lineal walk along a ridge, past three tors, to a stone circle. Length:
½ miles/8.8km *(there and back); Height Climbed:* **720ft/220m**.
B: *The stone circle is in a firing range* – see Introduction.

O.S. Sheet OL28

reach the start of this walk drive
½ miles east from Tavistock on
e B3357. Shortly after the road
nerges from fields onto the open
oor there is a large car park to the
ght of the road, but this is a short
stance from the start of the walk. If
ere is room, therefore, park in the
ext (small) car park, to the left of the
ad beyond a stream.

From the back of the small car
ark, take a grassy path through gorse
d bracken, heading straight for
Iiddle Staple Tor, visible above. The
ath leads up to the rocks, through
em, then on along the ridge to the
rger Great Staple Tor.

Beyond, continue to the final tor
Roos Tor – where there is a flag-
ole. If a flag is flying, you will not
e able to continue to the stone circle.
there is no flag, continue along the
dge on a clear, damp path. The path
ps to a low point, crosses a line of
d and white poles (the boundary
the range) then climbs gently to
angstone Moor stone circle – sadly
amaged by target practice during
World War II.

Double back along the same route.
you parked at the main car park
en you can drop off the ridge be-
ween Roos Tor and Great Staple Tor
reach a small tarn. A path leads
om there directly to the car park.

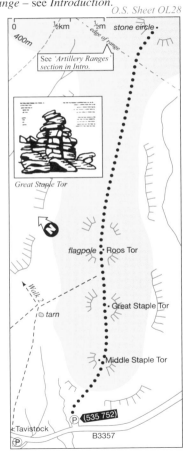

0   ½km   ½m   stone circle

400m   edge of range

See 'Artillery Ranges'
section in Intro.

Great Staple Tor

flagpole • Roos Tor

Great Staple Tor

Walk 2

tarn

Middle Staple Tor

P (535 752)

Tavistock

P

B3357

4 Great Mis Tor

A short, straight climb, largely on a clear track, to a fine tor and viewpoint. Length: **3 miles/5km** (there and back); Height Climbed: **525ft/160m**.

To reach the start of this walk, drive 5 miles east from Tavistock on the B3357 road for Princetown. The car park is a mile beyond Merrivale and is unmistakable – it is down to the right of the road, surrounded by walls topped by beech trees.

A path leads south from the car park towards King's Tor (*see* Walk 6), but for this walk cross the road (carefully) and walk right for a short distance to reach the start of a clear track.

The track leads up the slope to Little Mis Tor then stops. Beyond this a rough footpath continues to the more extensive Great Mis Tor – one of the most dramatic of the Dartmoor tors.

Note the flagpole on the tor. As you climbed you would have noticed a line of red and white posts encroaching from the right. These mark the edge of the army firing range. If a flag is flying on the post, the range is in use. (Even if the flag is not flying, walkers should be careful not to touch any suspicious objects they find within these areas – they may be live ordnance.)

Enjoy the fine views northwards, into the heart of Dartmoor, and west to Great Staple Tor and Roos Tor (Walk 3), and north-west to White Tor (Walk 1).

Retrace your steps to the car park.

Little Mis Tor

Vixen Tor _____ B

_moderate circuit on rough paths over open ground, passing the
splendid Vixen Tor._ **NB**: _the tor itself is on private ground and cannot be
approached._ _Length:_ **3 miles/5km**; _Height Climbed:_ **165ft/50m**.

O.S. Sheet OL28

To reach the start of this walk, drive
east from Tavistock on the B3357.
On the moor, at the end of the first
climb, there is a large car park to the
right of the road. Drive past this, and
one more smaller car park to the left,
and park in the second car park to
the left.

Cross the road and a path starts
directly opposite, passing through
clumps of gorse with the distinctive
tor directly ahead. After a short distance the path crosses another. Head
half-right on this new path, which
leads directly to a bridge over a leat.

Cross the bridge and follow a path
into the valley beyond, then back up
the other side to rejoin the leat, near
a stone cross. Go half-left from here,
following a path away from the leat
and up a low hill to reach a small tor
(Feather Tor).

Beyond the tor continue in the
same direction – on any one of a
number of paths – to reach the larger
Pew Tor, visible ahead. From the top
here is a fine view southwards.

Walk left along the tor then
descend to join a clear path running
along above a wall around fields,
visible below. Follow the path by
the wall (avoid cutting corners; the
ground is marshy) to reach the wall
around Vixen Tor. Admire the view
but don't enter – it is private ground.

Follow the wall to the far side of
the tor. A path continues by the wall,
but to complete this walk follow
another path, straight up the moor
– aiming slightly to the left of Middle
Staple Tor, beyond the road. This
leads you back across the leat and up
to the car park.

6 Princetown to King's Tor

*A lineal walk leading to a circuit of King's Tor, passing old quarries. Follows a clear track along an old railway line. Leaflet available from information centre. Length: **6 miles/9.6km**; Height Climbed: negligibl*

O.S. Sheet OL

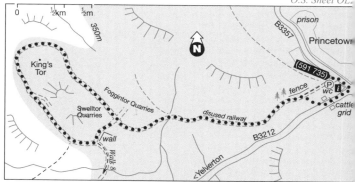

Park in the large car park in Princetown. Walk past the High Moorland Visitor Centre and on to the main road junction in the village. Turn right, beside the B3212 Yelverton road.

The road leaves the village, crosses a cattle-grid then passes between two houses. Just beyond the right-hand house there is a sign for a bridleway and a rough track starts.

Follow the track across to a fence, where it joins a clearer track, then continue; briefly with a wood to the right and then across the grassy moor. You are now on the old railway line – built originally to transport granite from the quarries in the 1820s, and later adapted for passenger transport until it was closed in the 1950s.

After a mile/1.6kms the track

swings right. You are now amongst the quarry workings. A track comes in from behind-left (your return route and heads off ahead-right. It is worth exploring the works (with care). Having done so, return to the line and continue.

The track makes an arc around King's Tor then doubles back down the far side of the hill. A grassy track heads off ahead-left. This leads into further quarry works. For this route, stick to the main track.

Beyond the quarry a clear track heads off to the left, uphill, with the remains of an old wall to the right. This edges right at the corner of the wall then continues to reach the junction with the track noted before. Turn right to return to the start.

Princetown to Siward's Cross _____ **B**

moorland path to a medieval cross, returning by an old leat and a quiet public road. Leaflet available from information centre. Length: **miles/9.5km**; *Height Climbed:* **165ft/50m**.

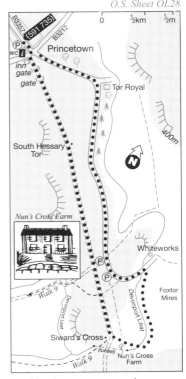

O.S. Sheet OL28

ark in the large car park in Princtown. Walk past the High Moorland isitor Centre and down to the road nction. Cross the road in front f you and go not right or left but traight on, with the Plume of Feathrs Inn to your right.

Follow a track between car parks o a gate, beyond which a clear path ontinues. At the next gate the walls nd to the right and you are on the pen moor.

Follow this good path, ignoring aths to right and left, for 2 miles/ .2km to the dramatic Siward's Cross an ancient boundary marker – then ead half-left, towards Nun's Cross arm. Pass to the left of the farm now a bunkhouse) and you will find ourself on a rough path with a wall o your left.

Follow this downhill to join the Devonport Leat (constructed in the 790s to provide water for the Devonort dockyards), which is joined just efore it vanishes into a tunnel (*see* Walk 10). Walk down the right-hand ide of the leat, noting Foxtor Mires o your right (supposed inspiration for Grimpen Mire in *The Hound of the Baskervilles*).

When a quiet public road crosses he leat, join the road and turn left. t is possible to follow this road all he way back to Princetown. If you would rather return across the moor, watch for the second car park to the left of the road and turn left, on a clear track, leading uphill to your original path.

8 Walkhampton Loop

A complex circuit on grassy paths and rough tracks, over open moorland, through farmland, and along the bed of a disused railway. Possible link with Walk 6. Length: **6¹/₂ miles/10.4km**; *Height Climbed:* **395ft/120m**.

O.S. Sheet OL2

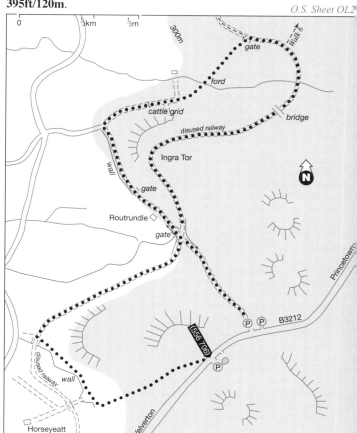

reach the start of this walk, drive
miles south from Tavistock on the
386, to Yelverton. At the rounda-
ut turn left on the B3212 and fol-
w it for 3 miles as it climbs on to
e moor. Once you are on the moor,
atch for a small pond to the right of
e road. Park either at the car park
re, or at the larger car parks slightly
rther along, to the left of the road.

Cross the road from the pond and
u will see a yellow arrow, pointing
f to the left. This marks the start of
theoretical footpath. In fact, there
no clear path. Just walk down the
ope through scattered gorse, edging
ay from the road, until you reach
wall along the top of fields. Turn
ght and walk across the slope with
e wall to your left.

A deep V in the walls marks the
ne of the right of way. Ignore that
d continue above the walls until
e bed of an old railway comes out
the fields to your left and crosses
wooden footbridge. Turn right
ong the old line – built originally
transport granite from the quarries
King's Tor in the 1820s, and later
apted for passenger transport until
was closed in the 1950s.

Follow the line across the slope for
st under a mile/1.6km until a track
osses from back-right to ahead-left
d a fence comes up from the left to
n by the track. Go left on the track
reach a gate marked by a bridleway
gn. Beyond the gate, continue on a
ne between walls, passing a house
ong the way (Routrundle).

The track reaches a gate, beyond

which there is a wall only to the left.
Continue like this until the wall and
path turn left and go downhill to join
a clear track, extending from a public
road which ends just to your left.
Turn right along this track.

Follow this track over a cattle-grid
in the line of a wall. Shortly beyond
this a grass track heads off to the
right. Ignore this, but when the main
track bends left, just beyond, look
for a sign for a footpath to your right.
The path, through gorse, is narrow
and damp, but the route is clear. It
leads to a ford over a small stream (if
the stream is in spate, there is a place
to jump over a little upstream).

The next section is not always
clear. The path continues, through
scattered gorse, with a broken-down
wall off to the left. The path then becomes less clear. When the wall pulls
away to the left, keep straight on.
In a short way the path edges to the
right and climbs, passing through an
old wall, to reach a gate in the fence
running beside the old railway. (If
you miss the path and there is no gate
when you reach the fence, just check
to left then right until you find it.)

Once through the gate turn right
along the railway line. A clear track
quickly turns off to the left (see Walk
6), but for this route keep straight
on until you return to the junction at
which you originally left the line.

Turn left and follow a clear path
over the low hill and back to the large
car parks by the road. Turn right
along the verge for a short distance to
return to the car park by the pond.

9 Burrator to Siward's Cross /
10 Burrator & Devonport Leat ———— A/A

Two linked walks through the woods and moorland to the east of Burrator Reservoir. **9)** *A modest climb to a tor and a pathless ridge walk to an old cross, with a return along a clear track.* Length: **5¹/₂ miles/8.8km**; Height Climbed: **620ft/190m**. **10)** *A brief climb on a moorland track and a return by an old leat, through moorland and mixed woodland. Paths damp in places.* Length: **4 miles/6.4km**; Height Climbed: **490ft/150m**.

O.S. Sheet OL2

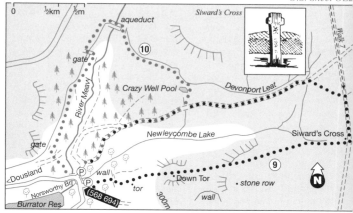

To reach Burrator Reservoir, drive 4 miles south from Tavistock on the A386 to Yelverton. At the roundabout turn left (B3212). After a mile you reach Dousland. Turn right here and follow the signs for the reservoir. In a little over a mile you reach the dam. Keep straight on here and continue until you cross the narrow Norsworthy Bridge beyond the head of the reservoir. Park either just beyond the bridge or in the car park immediately beyond a second bridge, just ahead.

Walk 9) This walk starts from the second car park. Start up the clear track behind the car park but turn left, almost immediately, on an unsignposted grassy footpath through bracken. (The next section is a confusion of paths and old walls – just remember that you are climbing to Down Tor and keep going uphill).

Pass through a gap in an old wall and continue to the top-right corner of the next field. Cross the corner of the next field to a gap in a wall then continue through bracken, with a wall off to the right. This leads to a gap in a wall with a T-junction of paths just beyond.

Go right and follow the rough path to the first small tor. Beyond, a rough path leads on to the craggy top of Down Tor, visible ahead. Walk to the far (east) end and the path disappears.

Looking ahead you see a ridge covered in tussocky grass. There is a valley down to the left (Newleycombe Lake) and a wall bending away to the right. You can aim straight up the near side of the ridge or edge right to see the stone row and cairns on the far side. Navigationally, just watch for the fork in the valley of New-leycombe Lake, after a mile/1.6km. Walk up the right-hand side of the right-hand valley and a clear path leads to Siward's Cross, on the water-shed by a clear path.

This 7ft/2m cross is an ancient boundary marker. Ahead-right you will see Nun's Cross Farm (see Walk 7), but for this walk go left, along the clear path.

Follow the path for a little under 1/2 mile/0.8km to reach a four-way junction (unsignposted). Go left. In a short way you join a clear track, com-ing in from behind-right, just before crossing Devonport Leat. Follow this track down the valley. A mile/1.6km from the leat you cross a stream. To link with Walk 10, go right; otherwise continue down the valley – keeping left at the two clear junctions – to return to the start.

Walk 10) Start this walk up the clear track in line with the end of Norsworthy Bridge, with a wood to your left. Almost immediately a track heads off to the left. Keep straight on. 1/2 mile/0.8km further on another track heads left. Keep straight on again, with the trees to your left.

The track leaves the trees behind. Shortly beyond it crosses a small stream. Immediately beyond this a rough path climbs to the left. Follow this uphill to Crazy Well Pool, then continue straight uphill to reach Devonport Leat – part of a network of granite millstreams built in the 1790s to supply water to the Devonport dockyards.

Turn left along the leat (either side will do at this point) and continue for a mile/1.6km to reach a steep descent to the aqueduct over the River Meavy. A rather flimsy wooden platform to the right of the watercourse allows you to cross the aqueduct (it is sound at time of writing; if it looks dodgy just ford the river).

Follow the leat to the edge of a wood. Cross the footbridge to reach a gate (sign: Crossgate) and continue, through the trees, to the left of the leat.

You reach a signposted junc-tion. Go straight on (Crossgate). A little way further on you go through a pedestrian gate beside a larger gate. Just beyond the gate veer left on a track, away from the leat. You quickly reach a signposted junction. Go left (Norsworthy Bridge).

You quickly reach a track. Go straight across to find a gate, then fol-low the path downhill, through dense woodland, to return to the start.

Walks South Dartmoor

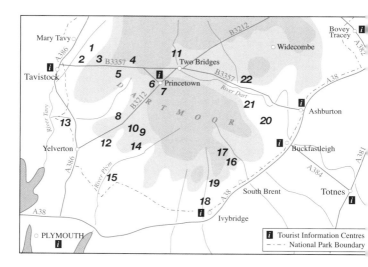

Grades

A ...... Full walking equipment required. Underfoot conditions occasionally wet or rough and some navigation may be needed

B ...... Strong walking footwear and waterproof clothing required. Underfoot conditions generally good and navigation largely straightforward.

C ...... Comfortable walking footwear recommended.

— www.pocketwalks.com —

Published by: Hallewell Publications, The Milton, Foss, Pitlochry PH16 5NQ

Printed by: J Thomson Printers, Glasgow

Walks South Dartmoor

11 Wistman's Wood & The Tors

A lineal route up a valley to a splendid wood of dwarf oaks, then along a line of three tors. The paths are rough but the route straightforward.
Length: 5 miles/8km *(there and back)*; **Height Climbed: 610ft/185m.**

O.S. Sheet OL2

Start this walk from Two Bridges – a mile north-east of Princetown at the junction of the B3212 and the B3357. If you are arriving from the west, cross the bridge over the West Dart River and turn left into the car park.

Start walking along the track from the back of the car park; quickly passing through a gate then continuing with a wall to the left. The track leads up to the house at Crockern. Keep to the right of the house grounds and continue up the valley of grass and gorse on a rough path.

Just beyond, the path splits as it approaches a wall. Either will do; they rejoin beyond the wall then continue up the valley to the National Nature Reserve of Wistman's Wood: an almost impenetrable area of stunted, twisted oak trees growing from between mossy boulders.

The path runs along the top of the wood. At the end of the wood it becomes fainter. It is possible to return from this point, but if you wish to extend the walk take a faint path leading straight up the slope to your right to the rocks of Longaford Tor.

Head left from the dramatic rocks and a path leads along the ridge to the smaller Higher White Tor. Just beyond is a wall with a stile over it. Cross this to continue to Lower White Tor, visible ahead.

Return by the same route.

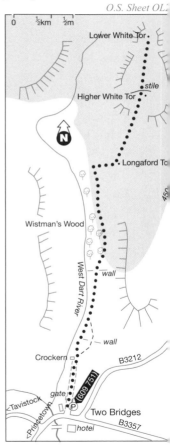

*A short, simple circuit over an area of grassland and gorse, following grassy paths and rough tracks. Length: 2¹/₂ **miles/4km**; Height Climbed: **230ft/70m**.*

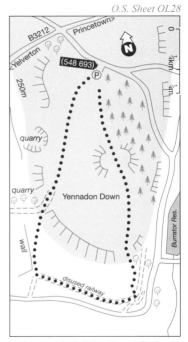

O.S. Sheet OL28

Yennadon Down is immediately to the west of Burrator Reservoir. To reach it, drive 4 miles south from Tavistock on the A386 to Yelverton. At the roundabout turn left (B3212). After a mile you reach Dousland. Keep straight on for a further ¹/₂ mile then turn first right, onto a minor road which heads off at the far end of an area of woodland. The car park is a short way up this road, to the right, on the near side of a conifer plantation.

Standing in the car park with your back to the road, you will see a grassy path heading off ahead-right. Start off along this, following the strongest path (it splits and reforms constantly) through grassland and scattered gorse.

After a little over ¹/₂ mile/0.8km a tongue of trees comes up from the right, in an old quarry. Keep to the left of this, and when the main path swings right just beyond, keep straight on instead, joining the line of a gorse-covered boundary wall to your right.

Continue down to the bottom corner of the wall, crossing a footbridge over an old mill leat on the way, then keep straight on for a short distance to meet a junction with a clear track. Go left along this – the bed of an old railway.

Follow this track across the slope until it swings left, approaching trees, and joins with another track coming

in from behind-right. Turn left along this for a few paces then leave it to the left on a rough, clear path.

Follow this path uphill. There are a mass of paths heading off to right and left, but keep climbing – running roughly parallel to the edge of the woods to your right – and the path will take you back to the car park.

An undulating, low-level circuit through grazing land and fine mixed woodland in a river valley. Paths are numerous, so some care needs to be taken with navigation Length: **5 miles/8km**; Height Climbed: **330ft/100m**.

O.S. Sheet OL2

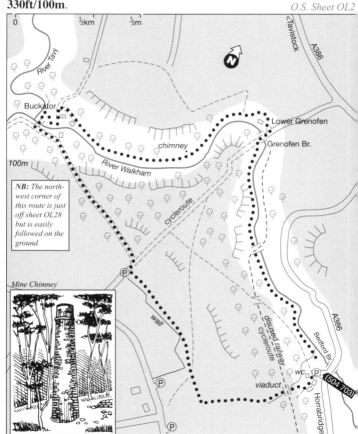

he grazing land and woodland
ound the River Walkham, west of
orrabridge and Yelverton, is a fine
ace for rambling and exploration.
he route given is one option, but
glance at the map, or a visit to the
e, will suggest many alternatives.

There are a number of car parks
the area (*see* map). For this route,
ive 2 miles south from Tavistock
the A386, until the road turns right
d crosses the River Walkham (Bed-
rd Bridge). Turn right immediately
yond, into the car park.

There are two connected car parks.
om the one nearer the road, look for
clear, signposted track which ini-
lly has a house to the left. Follow
is a short distance uphill until, level
th the last house to the left, it splits.
right and the path leads you under
e viaduct which once carried a
ilway line (if you reach the line, you
ve missed the junction).

Under the viaduct you are in a
allow valley. Cross the little stream
join a rough path up the valley.
u are in woods at present, but
ickly emerge into a wide area of
ass and bracken, criss-crossed by
ths. Continue roughly up the line
the valley. Whichever path you are
it will ultimately lead you to the
p of the slope. Veer left and you hit
e public road; veer right and you
in a wall (*see* map). Wherever you
e, go right, to walk along gently
scending grassland with the wall to
ur left (sign: West Devon Way).

After ¹/₂ mile/0.8km a clear track
osses your way, with a small car

park to your left. Go right along this
road. Immediately it splits, with a
grassy cycle track going straight on.
Keep left, on the main track, and follow it down and across the slope into
wooded parkland.

After a little under a mile/1.6km
the track reaches the River Walkham.
Double back for a short distance to
reach a footbridge over the river. This
is a pleasant, wooded spot, with rocky
outcrops, just above the confluence
of the Walkham and the Tavy. Once
over the bridge keep left and walk a
short distance up the Tavy to reach a
three-way junction.

Go right, crossing a saddle over
the rocky outcrop, to join the path
through the woods by the Walkham.
The path quickly pulls away from
the river to pass to the left of a house
(Buckator). Turn left up the driveway, which climbs in an S-bend.

After a short climb you reach a
signposted junction. Go right, off the
metalled road (bridleway). You now
have a walk of a mile by the river,
through trees, passing the chimney of
an old mine along the way.

You reach a pedestrian gate
(bridleway) then edge left beyond,
to bypass a house down to the right
(Lower Grenofen). That leads you
round to the entrance to the house
then on down the driveway.

When the driveway joins a metalled road, go right to cross Grenofen
Bridge. On the far side turn left and
follow a path through the woods by
the river for a mile/1.6km, back to the
car park.

14 Eylesbarrow Mine

A circuit over the open moor, passing splendid archaeological remains – ancient cairns and standing stones and a 19th-century tin mine – and following the upper waters of the River Plym. Paths are rough and can be wet in places. Some navigation needed. Length: **5¹/₂ miles/8.8km**; *Height Climbed:* **430ft/130m**.

O.S. Sheet OL2

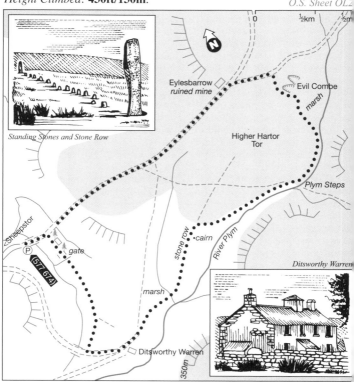

Standing Stones and Stone Row

Eylesbarrow ruined mine

Evil Combe

marsh

Higher Hartor Tor

Plym Steps

stone row

•cairn

River Plym

Ditsworthy Warren

Sheepstor

P (577 674)

gate

marsh

350m

Ditsworthy Warren

Eylesbarrow is a disused tin mine in the moors to the east of Burrator Reservoir. To reach the start of this walk

to it, drive 4 miles south from Tavistock on the A386 to Yelverton. At the roundabout turn left (B3212). After a ile you reach Dousland. Turn right ere, onto a minor road, following e signs for the reservoir. When you each the dam go right, over the dam, n the road to the village of Sheeps- or. Keep straight on through the illage, following the sign for Nattor : the last junction and continuing to e end of the public road.

Cross a cattle-grid then park to e right, just beyond; just before a ream. Start walking along the track hich crosses the stream. There is stand of trees around a building, isible ahead. Half way up the side f this plantation there is a gate to our right and a sign for a bridleway. ere you have a choice – if you just ant to visit the mine, keep straight 1; if you wish to do the whole walk, o right.

Follow the path in front of the uilding and continue to reach a ate on the far side of the enclosure. eyond this you cross a small stream en continue across the slope on a rassy path through bracken, with a ream down to your right. The path ips and then splits. Keep right and ollow the path to a junction with a ear track visible to your right, just fter the track has crossed the stream.

Turn left along the track to reach e empty farm at Ditsworthy War- n. Go left, on the near side of the rm, on a clear, rough track. The ack leads up the side of the valley f the River Plym. Looking ahead, ou should be able to see two large llars on a grassy hillside, with a ath leading straight to them. That is

your route, but you may get wet feet crossing the marshy stream at the foot of the slope.

The stones are the most visible part of a rich array of ancient archeology, including settlements, stone rows and cairns. Walk to the nearest standing stone (the tallest on the site is around 14ft/4m) and up the stone row beyond, passing a large cairn on the way (the Giant's Basin). At the tall stone beyond the cairn, edge right on a grassy path to continue up the river valley.

You reach a clear split in the river (by the Plym Steps ford) and a clear path comes in from behind-left. Ignore this and continue up the side of the valley. The path now becomes rougher and the valley narrower, before opening out into a broad, marshy area.

Go left, around the edge of the marsh, until a forked valley heads off to your left (Evil Combe). Take the path up the left-hand side of the left-hand valley. At the top you find a faint path running across your route. Turn right along this, climbing gently, for a short distance to join a clear track.

Turn left along this for a short distance to reach a junction amidst the ruins of the buildings of Eylesbarrow Mine. The remaining walls are low (the mine ceased operations in 1852), but the surrounding ground is still pitted with mounds and pits, and care must be taken when exploring.

Go left at the junction and follow the clear track back to the start.

A circuit through fine mixed woodland and open grassland around a narrow river valley, leading to a famous viewpoint. Steep in places.
Length: **4 miles/6.5km**; *Height Climbed:* **560ft/170m**.

O.S. Sheet OL2

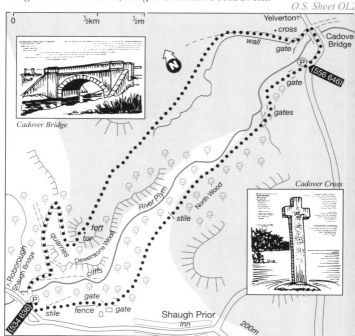

Cadover Bridge

Cadover Cross

The Dewerstone is the name given to the massive, dramatic crags overlooking the River Plym where it squeezes through a narrow, wooded valley. At the top of the crag is a viewpoint, in what was once an Iron Age fort.

There are car parks at either end of this walk. The walk can be started from Cadover Bridge (follow

the signs from Yelverton), but this description starts from the car park at Shaugh Bridge. To reach it, drive north from Plymouth on the A386. Roborough is on the edge of the city. Just beyond the large roundabout at the north of the town turn right (east) on the minor road for Shaugh Prior. Follow this road for 3 miles and it

...osses Shaugh Bridge. Just beyond ...ere is a car park to the left.

At the end of the car park furthest ...om the bridge there is a sign for a ...ath to Cadover Bridge. Climb steps, ...tting off a corner of the road, then ...rn left at another sign, following a ...ootpath through the woods.

The path quickly climbs to a stile ...ver a fence, beyond which the path ...plits. Go right here (note the yellow ...ots on the trees). Paths head left, ...to the wooded den, but you climb ... a fence and continue with that to ...our right to reach a gate near some ...ouses. Go through the gate and con-...nue between the fence and a house.

This leads to another gate, beyond ...hich you continue across the ...ooded slope on a rough path. The ...ath follows the line of an old pipe-...ne, which is occasionally visible on ...e path. Looking left, you may catch ...ccasional views of the cliffs on the ...r side of the valley.

The path crosses an open area to ...ach a stile over an old wall, beyond ...hich you are in North Wood – a ...ational Trust property. Follow the ...ath through the wood. Immediately ...ter leaving it you cross a footbridge ...ver a stream then pass through two ...tes in quick succession.

The path starts with a fence to the ...ght, at the top of a wood, then de-...ends across the slope to reach a gate ... the edge of the trees. The Cadover ...ridge car park is visible ahead, with ...e bridge beyond.

Go through the car park, over the ...idge (it is narrow; be careful of traf-...c) and climb a short distance beyond

to reach a junction, with tracks heading off from the road to right and left.

Go left. As the track approaches a gate in a wall head right, uphill (passing a cross on the way), beside the wall. The wall quickly turns to the left and runs along the slope. You can either follow the wall or climb further to the right to follow one of the other paths through this open grazing land. Either way, when the wall turns back down the slope you keep straight on, down the top of the ridge, to reach the small tor at the top of the Dewerstone – a terrific viewpoint.

Having admired the view (and the incised lettering in the rock) keep straight on in the same direction (don't go left – remember the cliffs). The path crosses the line of an old wall then edges down to the right, through very fine mature oakwood.

It joins the end of a grassy track, built into the slope – one of the access tracks to the old quarries. You reach a hairpin bend with an old structure beyond it. Double back down the slope; the track now partly paved.

Come down to a junction with a track running across the slope. Go ahead-left. This leads you to a fork. Go ahead-right, downhill. Almost immediately you reach a hairpin bend, beyond which the track is entirely paved.

A path heads off back-left, with a map at the junction. This lineal path gives access to the foot of the crags, but is a bit of a scramble at its far end. To complete the circuit, keep straight on at the junction to reach a footbridge and the car park, just beyond.

16 Avon Dam / 17 Avon Dam & Brent Moor___C/A

16) *A straightforward lineal walk, on a metalled road, up a picturesque valley to a dam and reservoir. Length:* **4 miles/6.4km** *(to the dam and back); Height Climbed:* **395ft/120m**. **17)** *An extension of the previous walk, leading onto the moors and back by an old tramway. There are no paths in places, so some navigation will be needed. Length:* **8 miles/ 12.8km**; *Height Climbed:* **820ft/250m**.

O.S. Sheet OL2

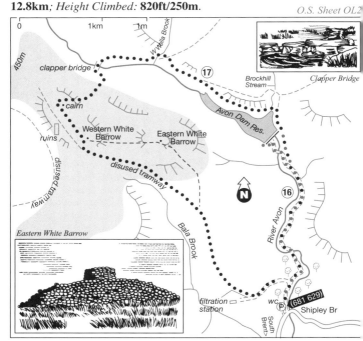

To reach the start of these walks, drive 4 miles east from Ivybridge on the A38 to reach the village of South Brent. From here, follow the signs for Shipley Bridge for around 2 miles, through a maze of minor roads, to

reach the car park beside the bridge.

Walks 16 & 17) Walk past the toilets and you quickly join a metalled road running up the left-hand side of the River Avon through mature woodland and rhododendrons. After

short distance there is a junction
with a second road. Keep right, by
the river.

The road leaves the trees, crosses
the river and continues through moorland. Shortly after catching your first
sight of the dam the road crosses a
stream, begins to climb and reaches a
junction, with an unmade track heading up to the right.

Walk 16) If you go right at this
point, the track leads you to the edge
of the reservoir. If you continue by
the road, it leads to the foot of the
dam (a path then leads up to the far
end of the reservoir). Please note that
you cannot cross the reservoir.

Return by the same route.

Walk 17) For the longer route, go
right and follow the rough track to the
end of the dam. Just before you reach
the dam, go right on a rough footpath
which leads along the edge of the
reservoir.

After crossing Brockhill Stream
the rough path edges away from the
reservoir, gently climbing to join a
slightly clearer path just beyond the
head of the reservoir. Follow this up
the side of the valley.

The main valley bends left and a
tributary valley comes in from the
right (Western Wella Brook). It is
marshy around the confluence, so
edge right to find a place to cross the
brook then double back down the far
side on a faint path. Beyond the confluence, continue up the right-hand
side of the River Avon.

In $1/2$ mile/0.8km you reach the
upper bridge over the river. Cross

this, climb a little way up the slope
beyond, then turn left across the
slope. There is no path; just continue
until you reach a rough path, crossing
your route. Turn right along this.

The path follows the edge of a
shallow, marshy corrie, then starts
climbing to the right of an obvious
grassy gully. At the top, turn left on
a faint path. This quickly disappears
– just keep straight on to join the
ridge ahead, near a cairn with a stone
standing in it.

Turn left along the ridge, towards
the distinctive Western White Barrow,
noting the ruined mine buildings
below to your right and the two old
tramways. You will ultimately be
following the upper of the two (ie, the
fainter one, above the ruins).

At this point you have a choice.
If visibility is poor, drop down to
the right to join the line of the old
tramway (faint in places) and follow
it down into the valley of Bala Brook.
If it is clear, continue along the ridge
(be careful of the mine workings) to
the distinctive Eastern White Barrow.
Beyond the Barrow, follow a faint
path down the nose of the hill. Continue until you are walking through
short, cropped grass then turn right,
off the path, to join the tramway.

Either way, the lower tramway is
very clear, descending in an 'S' bend
to reach the wall above the Filtration
Station. Go left – staying above the
thickest gorse – to reach the metalled
access road, then follow it down to
the junction with the Avon Dam road.

Turn right to return to the start.

A short loop on clear tracks, steep in places, through the woods of the Erme Valley. Length: **1-2 miles/1.6-3.2km**; *Height Climbed:* **200ft/60n**

O.S. Sheet OL2

Ivybridge is the largest town on the southern edge of Dartmoor – 4 miles east of the edge of Plymouth on the A38. There is a pay car park in the centre of the town. Alternatively, there is limited parking by Station Road, near the start of the path.

If you are starting this walk from the town centre, find your way to the roads running up the left-hand side of the River Erme (ie, going upstream). Towards the edge of the town this is Station Road.

Station Road edges left and there is a bridge crossing the river to your right and a gate into a park to your left. Just beyond the bridge there is a sign to the right of the road marking the start of a path. Follow this path through trees, with a series of rapids in the river down to the right.

The path passes under an enormous Victorian railway viaduct (note the second set of piers from an earlier structure). 30m beyond there is a junction with a track. Go back-left on this, back under the viaduct to a gate leading on to the public road.

Turn right, along the road. Ignore two roads going left and keep straight on up the metalled road, passing a house to your left. Before you reach the top of the climb there is an entrance to the right, leading in to a flat area. Immediately beyond this a path starts to the right.

Follow this clear path down and

across the slope into the wooded valley. At the bottom of the slope you join the clear path up the valley. Explore upstream as far as you wish but to return to the start turn right an follow the clear path back to the first junction above the viaduct.

*gentle climb to a ridge with fine views and archaeological remains,
nd a return past ancient hut circles. Length:* **4¹/₂ miles/7km**; *Height
limbed:* **430ft/130m.**

O.S. Sheet OL28

o reach the start of this walk from
ybridge, find Harford Road, which
arts in the town centre, and follow
out of the town and north for a
rther 2 miles to reach the hamlet of
arford. Turn right at the junction
efore the church (Harford Moor) and
llow a narrow public road to a gate.
here is parking on the moor-edge,
st beyond.

Walk out the back of the parking
ea. There is a faint path, but if you
n't find it don't worry: just aim
raight up the slope, keeping above
e valley down to your right.

Just short of the ridge a path
ns across the slope, along a line of
oundary stones. Turn left along this,
wards a low, rounded hilltop. You
ıss a stone with an incised cross and
en the slanting Longstone. Contin-
a short distance beyond this until
e path joins a clear track.

Obviously it is possible to extend
our walk along the ridge for some
stance, but for this walk dou-
e back along the track. After ²/₃
ile/1km there is a split by a small
ond. A brief diversion to the left
ads to Spurrell's Cross.

Return to the track and follow it
rough the line of boundary stones.
path follows the line of stones, to
e left. For this route continue on the
ack until a path heads left, straight
r Hangershell Rock tor.

Turn right to return to the track
and continue. The track makes a wide
curve around Weatherdon Hill. At the
point where it begins to turn left, head
straight downhill on a grassy path,
leading down the left-hand side of a
stand of conifers visible below.

Turn right at the bottom of the
plantation; crossing a stream and
passing through a group of very well
preserved Bronze Age huts. Continue
beyond, with a wall to your left, to
return to the start.

A moderate circuit, starting through farmland on metalled roads and clear tracks and climbing onto the edge of the moor. Some navigation will be needed on the moorland section. Length: **4¹/₂ miles/7.2km**; *Height Climbed:* **660ft/200m**.

O.S. Sheet OL

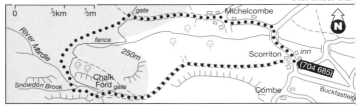

Scorriton is a tiny village with an inn on the east side of Dartmoor; 3 miles from Buckfastleigh on minor roads. Parking is very limited but there is room for a few cars in the centre of the village (make sure you don't block any entrances).

From the village, walk north on a minor road (narrow, so keep out of the way of any traffic) signposted for Michelcombe. The road descends to a bridge over a stream. Keep left at the junction just beyond to reach the village of Michelcombe.

Walk up through the village to reach a signposted junction. Go left here (bridleway only). After a short distance tracks head off first left then right, but you keep straight on at both junctions. Beyond this, follow the straight, clear track between walls as it climbs towards the moor.

At the top of the lane there is a metal gate, beyond which you are on the edge of the grassy moor. Some navigation will be needed here.

Start by heading half-left on a

grassy track. This quickly splits and you will have to start making decisions. Essentially you are walking slightly up and across the slope, shadowing the line of the fences around the fields down to your left, until you reach the edge of the deep valley of the River Mardle.

Turn left, on the top of the slope above the river, until a fence joins you to your left and the path becomes too rough to follow. At this point, edge down the slope to your right and find a place to ford the little river.

Walk down the far side until you reach the confluence with Snowdon Brook. Cross this and continue with the river to your left for a short distance to reach the footbridge at Chalk Ford.

Cross the bridge and go through the gate just beyond to join a clear lane. Half way down the lane edges right and an unsigposted track heads off to the left. Ignore this and follow the lane back down to the start of the walk.

short, simple walk around a small reservoir on good paths. Length:
½ miles/2.4km; Height Climbed: negligible.

O.S. Sheet OL28

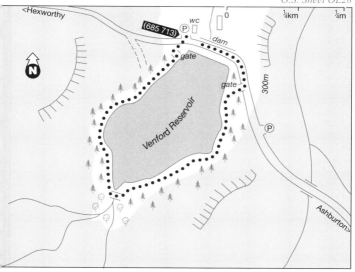

nford is a small reservoir on the
stern side of Dartmoor, surrounded
 mixed woodland. To reach it,
ive east from Two Bridges (a mile
rth of Princetown, at the junction
 the B3212 and the B3357) on
e B3357. After four miles a road
ads off to the right (if you reach the
idge at Dartmeet you have missed
 signposted for Hexworthy. Keep
 t at two junctions near Hexworthy
en continue for two miles along
e narrow road to reach a large car
rk to the left of the road at the near
d of the dam. (If this is full there

is another car park beyond the dam
– *see* map.)

The route could not be simpler.
Cross the road and go through the
second gate in an iron fence. This
leads to picnic tables and the start of
a path through the trees around the
reservoir.

Cross a footbridge at the top of the
reservoir then come down the other
side. A gate leads on to the public
road and you have to walk back
across the road/dam. Take some care
– this is narrow, but it can only be
avoided by retracing your steps.

22 Corndon Down

A moorland ridge walk passing ancient cairns, with fine views of the surrounding farmland. Rough paths and a quiet public road. Length: **4-4¹/₂ miles/6.4-7.2km***; Height Climbed: up to* **525ft/160m***.*

Two Bridges is a mile north-east from Princetown on the B3212. A further 4 miles east along the B3357 is the hamlet of Dartmeet. Follow the road up the slope beyond the bridge and you will pass a car park to the right of the road, at the highest point. Start either here or from the smaller car park by the monument (*see* map).

From the main car park, cross the road and start walking along a footpath which runs parallel. On the horizon, a cross is visible. When a clearer, grassy path crosses your way, turn left along this, now aiming for the cross.

The path reaches a minor road. Go left for a short distance to reach the path to the cross (a WWI memorial), then continue on a rough path to reach a small tor. Turn left, past a large cairn, towards a second hill, on which two large cairns are visible.

Pass between the cairns then continue along the ridge, gradually descending to join the public road at the point where a track heads off to the left. Walk a few paces along this track then leave it, walking ahead-left along a grassy track between low banks of bracken and gorse.

When the track splits, keep left. There is a wall around fields ahead. You should be at the top left-hand corner; if you are further down, follow the wall up to the corner and

continue – above the wall at first, th pulling away. The path soon joins the public road by the picturesque thatched houses at Sherwell.

Turn left along the quiet road to turn to the car park by the memorial